KRISTA BURLAE

BALBOA.
PRESS
A DIVISION OF HAY HOUSE

Balboa Press books may be ordered through booksellers or by contacting:

Balboa Press
A Division of Hay House
1663 Liberty Drive
Bloomington, IN 47403
www.balboapress.com
1-(877) 407-4847

Because of the dynamic nature of the Internet, any web addresses or links contained in this book may have changed since publication and may no longer be valid. The views expressed in this work are solely those of the author and do not necessarily reflect the views of the publisher, and the publisher hereby disclaims any responsibility for them.

The author of this book does not dispense medical advice or prescribe the use of any technique as a form of treatment for physical, emotional, or medical problems without the advice of a physician, either directly or indirectly. The intent of the author is only to offer information of a general nature to help you in your quest for emotional and spiritual well-being. In the event you use any of the information in this book for yourself, which is your constitutional right, the author and the publisher assume no responsibility for your actions.

Any people depicted in stock imagery provided by Thinkstock are models, and such images are being used for illustrative purposes only.
Certain stock imagery © Thinkstock.

Printed in the United States of America

ISBN: 978-1-4525-7013-6 (sc)
ISBN: 978-1-4525-7014-3 (e)

Balboa Press rev. date: 4/30/2013

I wrote this workbook because I've met so many people who have great stories to tell. I've spoken with women who've survived adverse treatment, men who've overcome great obstacles, and children who've been adopted and left abusive homes. The list is endless. For whatever reason, people tell me their stories. As they do, my mind spins with ideas about how to organize their memoir around the patterns I'm intuiting in their storytelling. I wrote it all down in the hopes that you can use it. Good luck presenting your story to the world.

To make *The Art of Cathartic Memoir* accessible to many, it is available online and in print. The online version is less expensive. However, there are portions of it that offer spaces for various prompts, exercises, and editing techniques should you purchase the print version. If you've purchased this online, you'll need a journal to complete those portions of the workbook.

Finally, writing cathartic memoir is no easy feat. Difficult emotions can arise that require support. Catharsis Writing Institute believes in rigorous training for coaches in the area of cathartic memoir that include academic degrees in teaching, counseling, or the fine arts and/ or training in artistic as well as personal sensitivity to this process. We will be offering a rigorous training program in the near future for people who'd like to use their expertise to offer you support. In the meantime, we have some highly skilled, trained coaches available to you if you are in need of support for your process. Please feel free to contact us for more information. If you just need a little support, we offer a community of other memoir writers through online chat and forum. Our community policies support the very delicate process of creating art from cathartic experience. Feel free to check out catharsisjournal.com to learn more about cathartic memoir and all that we offer to your writing process.

Foreword

Walk into any bookstore, and you'll find shelves packed with how-to and self-help books. It is a rare volume that combines the best of both genres. *The Art of Cathartic Memoir* does this, guiding people through the process of memoir writing as a means of cathartic healing. It teaches people how to write with examples and exercises, and it provides both inspiration and support for anyone struggling with the painful emotions that life experiences all too often generate.

If the volume is unique, so is its author. Krista Burlae of the Catharsis Writing Institute is singularly qualified to write such a book. An accomplished writer as well as a trained counselor, she skillfully draws on her own strengths to make her hard-won insights available to others. She has figured out over years of working with authors what tools aspiring memoir writers find most useful, and her own far-from-insignificant ability as a writer has allowed her to communicate methods and prompts in the pages that follow. Everyone has a story to tell; it takes a rare person like Krista, though, to provide a catalyst to allow that telling. I was privileged to be able to read some of the workbook in an early draft and found it—as well as Krista herself—deeply inspiring. I expect the finished volume to be even more so.

—Katherine Ulrich, PhD

KRISTA BURLAE

Table of Contents

Chapter 1: Overview

So, you've decided to write a book about your life. Congratulations for making this decision; it is a most laborious as well as rewarding process. If you are like most people who feel compelled to write a book, there is a little voice in your heart gnawing away at you until you complete the process. You may feel a strong urge to get your story out for a number of reasons. You may want to inform your family about long-lost secrets that will change their lives and heal wounds. You may have a really interesting story that others will find healing, transformative, or fascinating. You may have had a message from the divine, and you wish to make that message clear through writing about what you know. Whatever your reason, you will always have your completed book once you've achieved this monumental and worthwhile endeavor. You will have that piece of art that you leave as a legacy to family, clients, friends, and even the general public—and that little voice in your heart that says, "You need to write this book before you die," will be appeased. Ah, relief ...

A Little about the Writing Process

You probably already know this, but writing a book, especially a memoir, doesn't usually support you comfortably unless you are famous, or an extraordinary storyteller. Leave the door open for abundance and trust the process. Perhaps your book will lead you into the writing industry as an editor or coach, or it will allow you to know in your heart that you've followed a call and not denied an opportunity to be creative. The point is to have some financial resources available other than those from a future book, just in case you aren't famous or the next Augusten Burroughs, who wrote several books about his life with extraordinary skill.

You should understand the difference between essay, biography, and memoir. This book focuses on writing a memoir. Memoir is a more creative and reflective process than either essay or biography. Essay usually takes place in the present tense and reads more like a blog or diary. Often people write a series of essays in one book with a common theme, but they can be more loosely tied than a memoir and are less reflective of the past. Autobiography is the story of your life from birth to the day you stop writing it. Memoir captures a particular time, event, and theme in your life; it is usually a more creative process than biography. It can read like fiction, but has considerably less dialogue. Memoir uses the literary elements, whereas biography is more linear. Memoir can be structured in a less linear more artistic fashion, and you can build that structure from this workbook. You can also include childhood experiences when writing about an adult event. A typical memoir does not exceed 350 pages; plan for about 300.

Literary Elements

Writers use several literary elements, and you can search on the Internet to learn about them. However, some are especially juicy for memoir, and they are mentioned in the next chapter of this book. If you haven't had a course in literature, in which you recount some of the common literary elements used in writing, this chapter offers a strong comprehension of some basic elements. If you have knowledge of literary elements, you can let your creativity flow by reading how to apply them to memoir.

Organization

Some people can organize a story without first planning out a structure and without even trying. If you are that person, use this section to help you identify a new way of structuring your story, and refer to "Brainstorming" in chapter 4. Your best bet is to create your own structure, but this step is also what blocks many writers. Organizing your book is saying, "This is how I'm going to write it, the order in which I'll tell the story," and most people reading this get stuck when they even consider it. You don't have to follow the original structure you set if you find that you are going in a new and more exciting direction, but it is a starting point that offers you goals. Creative organizational designs are available here for you to choose the structure that best suits your personality and story. But as a creative person, you might feel most comfortable with your own design. Chapter 3 will offer more on these designs.

Creative Organizational Designs

Creative organizational designs are structures that give you a map of your book before you begin. In the structure, you create a section to be filled with content, and then you fill in the content. You have even more help from choosing your literary elements, which I'll ask you do next.

I offer six types of creative organizational designs that will allow you a structure for your story, but you are welcome to fashion your own if it works for you. Let your creative juices flow upon reading about this. The first and most common organizational design for a story is chronological, or by time (which is also under the literary element of setting). Others include by place, by character, therapeutic, spiritual, in medias res, and in fine; there are many other possibilities. Some of these are common ways of organizing a story; others are my own new and unique ways to organize books. I once worked with a client who had threes as a common theme in his story. Although he used chronology to organize his work, he decided he'd have 333 pages, and on every third chapter and page, something consistent would happen. That was his uniquely and creatively designed organization. In doing this, you can reach your reader on yet another level. Although they may not know it at first, you are offering them one more way of understanding how important a certain aspect of your story really is, and you are offering it on a level that is outside of normal cognitive comprehension. You hit your reader on a more basic level, whether or not she notices it.

Chronological

Most memoirs are told in chronological order, from beginning to end, and are demarcated by time (which is half of the setting). You can use seasons, months, specific dates, birthdates of characters, or whatever you wish, so long as the bulk of your story falls between two markers of time within life, but not birth to present. These demarcations of time can be included as either chapters or sections and chapters, but you should be consistent in what you use.

Place

Another way to organize your memoir is by place (the other half of the setting). I moved around a lot in a nomadic life, so this is how I will organize my memoir. Place has had a huge effect on me and how I've lived. Different places have different terrain, cultures, weather, lifestyle options, and so forth. If you have lived in the same place all of your life, you still move about to different places: work, home, leisure activities, homes of friends and relatives, and religious institutions. All of these places offer varying roles, emotions, and experiences. Furthermore, one reacts differently to all of these variables, and it's possible that various soul contracts are fulfilled in different places, not to mention specific forms of healing. How has place played a role in your emotional process?

Character

You can organize your memoir by its characters. Of course you still need to consider chronology, but in different way. I'll talk more about this in the next two chapters, but one of the best examples of this I've seen is Jodi Picoult's *My Sister's Keeper*. In this novel, she organizes the entire book by the characters and even has them dancing back in time to reveal things that need to be a part of the story.

Therapeutic

I recently read Jaycee Dugard's memoir, *A Stolen Life*. She uses a form of therapeutic organization mixed with chronological organization in her memoir. Every so often, after describing a particularly difficult period of her life (such as her first, forced sexual experience with her captor), she offers a "Reflection" section in which she as an adult makes sense of her ever-changing emotions about her own process. I'll offer more ideas of therapeutic memoir in chapter 3.

It's this process that we all share, with each of our experiences, that makes the therapeutic organization valuable. Furthermore, you might be writing about an adult event and can see childhood experiences that led you to that adult event in a particular way, thus showing a direct link from an early moment to a later one. Your *imprint*, if you will, is clearly understood by making this link in your book. You also can organize a therapeutic structure in other ways that I'll discuss later in the workbook.

Spiritual

The ways in which you can organize your memoir are boundless. If you are attached to a specific guru such as Eckhart Tolle, Carolyn Myss, Louise Hay, Debbie Ford, Wayne Dyer, or Don Miguel Ángel Ruiz, you can use their ideas to structure your life story. Or you may have a way of seeing the world all your own and wish to organize around this unique personal process that you carry with you. All personal processes of human beings are unique. They all carry potential infinite literary options with which you can work. They all carry elements of shadow and light on a continuum, as do we humans.

In Medias Res and In Fine

While hardly my original idea, these structures are ideal for memoirs about a specific catastrophic or exciting event. *In medias res* is Latin for "in the middle," and *in fine* translates as "at the end." As you apply this to your memoir, you can offer your event in all of its excitement at the beginning of your book to entice readers. The event may be the actual ending of your story, or it may be in the middle of your story. You can then backtrack in your work, tracing the steps of your life that led to the event.

Other Possibilities

Part of working out how to structure your memoir in this workbook will include identifying your own personal process with others and with the universe. After I've explained the above designs for your memoir, I'll offer information on how you can discover your own personal imprint and corresponding memoir structure.

Writer's Block and Tools to Help You Start and Keep Writing

One of the hardest things writers struggle with is simply getting started, whether it's getting started in the beginning or each time you sit down to write. You can do a number of things to celebrate this endeavor and keep yourself writing. To get started writing your book, I offer several ways in which you can rejoice in this commencement.

Implements and Accoutrement

Now that you've made this decision, treat yourself. Go out to your favorite bookstore and buy yourself a special pen or pencil that you adore. Try to choose the type of instrument you learned to write with when you were a child. If you learned to type instead of write by hand, because you were born in the computer age, then find a perfect background for your computer screen; choose one that inspires you. You'll be looking at it, and at times you'll need such inspiration. Whatever your original medium, get to know it, bless it, and honor it as your friend. You are going to need to have a good relationship either with your pencil or with your computer, but most likely both. Make sure you have paper around as well, if not a favorite journal.

Some people are very uncomfortable with writing but can spin a yarn orally that enchants and enthralls. If this is you, get a good digital voice recorder. Podcasts are just as useful as books, but you will still need a structure for your story. Just before I decided to create this workbook, a friend sent me a journal, and I started all of the sections of this book in that journal. I would write them down throughout the day until I felt like I had the general overview of what I wanted to say. Then I framed my organization of this workbook. Finally, as you will do, I started filling content within the sections I created.

Space

Like anything else you do, you have to have a place to do it. Whatever your arrangement, make your space special and totally yours for the duration of your weekly writing time. If you have a favorite relative who's crossed over, place an item he or she gave you in the space and write to him or her. Put up some pictures or articles of your spiritual choice in the space. If you are writing for future generations, make space for pictures of your children or grandchildren or others whom you mentor through your writing. Bless it, honor it, and make it your creative haven; make sure that it is totally yours for your writing time. Some people need to leave town. I tend to write best when I have few distractions and find spaces that are particularly isolated. If you can afford to hang out away from your home to avoid distractions and it works for you, great—but you don't have to fork over that money. You can create your writing haven anywhere that honors your personal preferences. Additionally, some people work better with noise and chatter all about them. There are plenty of wonderful coffee shops, restaurants, and outdoor venues to make your haven. You can take your pictures or a talisman with you for inspiration. Your space is a state of mind more than a place, but one that you must protect as very important once you embark upon this process.

Tools to Keep You Writing

Chapter 4 is dedicated to showing you what your limits may be with your own creativity and how you can overcome those limits. Almost all writers struggle with sitting themselves down each and every time they write and at the beginning of a project. You can integrate a number of rituals and tools into your practice of writing to start and keep yourself writing.

Workshopping and Editing

Once you've completed a first draft of a manuscript, or even a chapter or two, you can start workshopping and editing it with other people. Workshopping is getting feedback, usually while reading it aloud to others. The idea of workshopping is to help keep you writing. You can choose a writing partner or a group, but make sure you are ready to share what you've written.

Editing has many facets. The two that are most important in memoir are developmental editing and copyediting. You will know when you are ready to hire an editor by how you feel when you share your work and get feedback. In chapter 5, I'll offer both workshopping rules and an editing checklist that will help improve your manuscript.

The Steps of Writing Your Memoir

The first thing you might do is organize your book. Or, if you are the person who can organize without writing it down, you might brainstorm in a number of ways to get your ideas out and clear, and just start writing from that point each and every time. Once you organize a structure or brainstorm the ideas you intend to write about, you can list your literary elements and choose which ones will apply to your memoir. Finally, using the structure or ideas, the literary elements, your personal practice of overcoming writer's block, and a helpful editor, you can place the puzzle pieces together and write that book. That little voice in your heart will be so relieved. With each word you write, the voice will slip out of your heart and onto the page.

In order to organize your book, you need to understand traditional literary elements and how they play into memoir, so that you can use them accurately in this genre.

Chapter 2: *Traditional Literary Elements*

*W*riters use hundreds of literary elements and devices to enhance their work. For your initial writing purposes in this genre, seven basic literary elements and devices will suffice, and they are: theme, setting, characters, point of view, symbolism, plot, and conflict and climax. In memoir, it is wise to reduce dialogue unless you actually recorded it, as memory can only serve to a degree.

Theme

The theme of your memoir is the basic meaning of your story, most likely philosophical. Common themes are courage, abandonment, hope, success after hardship, and love. But your theme or themes (yes, there can naturally be more than one) can be whatever is real for your story. Augusten Burrows's memoir *Running with Scissors* has the theme of survival through hardship. Jeanette Walls's memoir *Glass Castle* has a similar theme. Both also suggest overcoming adversity.

Given that you've purchased a book about your unique memoir structure having to do with catharsis, you might have a theme that includes a dark night of the soul, a shamanic experience, a near death experience or another event that changed you. Symbolic death and rebirth happen throughout our lives. Elizabeth Kubler Ross' memoir, *The Wheel of Life: A Memoir of Living and Dying*, has the theme of the cycle of life right in its title. Further, you may write about something miraculous that occurred in your life, such as how your life was spared in a disaster, the birth of your beautiful and healthy child, how you overcame a health issue, or maybe an epiphany you had because of something in the natural world that occurred. There are endless possibilities about how you may have transformed your life through dark or light. If you don't know it as you begin, you will certainly know your theme as you write. Your writing partner, group, or editor will assist you in seeing when you offer your work for review.

If you are a fan of Carolyn Myss, your theme might be about sacred contracts. Sacred contracts are instances in which people, before they are born, form contracts with other souls to learn particular lessons. For example, you might contract with a particular type of family to learn lessons that will assist you in helping other people. If you follow the teachings of Don Miguel Ruiz, you might include a theme in which you release yourself from agreements you made long ago based upon another's poisonous words. There are numerous themes that you may choose for your memoir. More likely, they may unfold without much thought or choice on your part at all.

Theme in your memoir is like a thesis in a graduate school paper. Most every sentence in your book resonates with the theme.

Setting

Setting includes both time and place, and when you are writing your memoir, you can reveal each of these through description. For instance, although you may wish to simply state that you are talking about 1972, you might also wish to take your reader into 1972. What were the styles of the time you write about? What references to music can you include to jog a memory or suggest the feeling of the era? What political events were taking place, and how was this affecting you at that time? All of these elements of time are bases for building your story.

Time can be measured in a variety of ways. Perhaps you use the seasons to demarcate time in your memoir. Perhaps you use marriages—or as a friend of mine describes it, "three men ago." You could measure time by typical months or years, but life events don't usually unfold to perfectly match them. I will write more about measuring time in the "Chronological" section in chapter 3.

Setting is also place. You can write about cities, natural settings, houses, the inside of your car, workplaces, churches, or wherever you spent time during the time frame of your memoir. You may need to write about different countries and their culture, terrain, and politics. Your description in your memoir can support both time and place so that the reader can jump into it with you.

You will want to consider how many shifts in time and place are necessary for your memoir. I once edited a memoir written by a Jewish partisan of the Second World War. He moved around very often, but it worked for his memoir because that was the reality of living in the woods and having to uproot when danger e was astute in describing each living arrangement forests of Russia and Belarus, which brought it all home to the reader.

Or, you may choose to downplay setting. Why would you want to downplay setting? To mask information! You may not wish to hurt your still-living Great Aunt Edith by remarking about her past and how it relates to your memoir. You may wish to keep detailed city names out of your memoir, to keep from outing a gay cousin. Masking information by also choosing different names for characters, or using general terms such as "X" or "XY," also help you to tell the story as you experienced it without accusing another of a crime.

Character and Character Building

Building strong characters in writing is imperative for your story, especially a cathartic story in which relationships may be a prominent piece. Yet as mentioned above, masking a character can be a method you need to employ as well. It's a fine balance, and you can find that balance in your writing. Finally, you need to keep the number of your main characters to a minimum of about five if possible. Readers can only attach to so many people in one book, and you will confuse and alienate them if you choose to include several characters. Definitely do not include more than ten.

In order for readers to attach to particular characters, you need to make them real. This isn't so hard to do when you consider what is real about your characters. What are their mannerisms that you adore or find distasteful? For instance, I have a friend who sniffs and cocks head after nearly every other sentence she speaks. She is a wonderful person, but the mannerism is not something one can ignore! It defines her in some ways, as do her gallant travels about the globe; she ignores money issues and lives as she pleases as much as possible. She is also erudite and brilliant, and she is one of the finest writers I know. She has dark hair and seldom wears makeup. She's urban, not rural, and enjoys the city and all it has to offer her. Be sure to offer characteristics such as these instead of the typical "She was a teacher," which she was at one time. We often define people by their careers, yet people are so much more than a career. Ask yourself, what is the first thing you noticed about this person? What emotions did this person elicit when you met him or her? What did you learn about him or her as your relationship deepened? How did this person's personality traits complement or clash with your own? How did those complements and clashes help you to grow and transform?

What's more in character building is offering a sense of the relationship that you had (and may still have, though memoir is written in past tense) with this person. You want to share the internal emotions you experienced with the person. In my friendship with the above character, I immediately liked her. She had loads more opportunity in life than I'd ever experienced, but she made me feel like I could have that opportunity, never putting me down. When I encountered her, I felt like the world was my oyster if I just believed. She was an inspiration to my writing, paying close attention to my talent and assisting in bringing it forth when I was very young, long before I understood I could write.

But when is it prudent to downplay a character? Like setting, you can tell a story without giving away who the person is by not giving out such details. Consider the following example.

> *At first, my boss loved me. She nurtured me beyond what is normal. She raved about me. She carried on so much that I presumed a honeymoon was taking place that just might end. As her personality revealed her dark side, about ninety days after my tenure commenced, she began to give me clients with communicable diseases (someone with TB who was coughing), hostile natures, and dangerous histories. I decided to leave the position and give my notice. My boss sat upright in her chair, exclaiming that I never told her I wanted to leave the job. I thought to myself,* Well, that is the power I hold as an employee selling my labor. *I was raised to hold that information until I gave my notice so that I did not make my employer wonder if I was staying and make myself miserable, wondering if I'd get fired as a result. At this professional position, I was surprised that she expected me to tell her of my intentions regarding the job. People in positions of petty power take that power beyond what is necessary. It was my job to hold my power. I simply replied, "I don't recall reading anywhere in a job description that I owed you that kind of revelation." I returned to my office to wrap up my work, which would only be for thirty more days. I didn't have to take the new clients, given that I was leaving!*

In the above example, I share more of how I was feeling internally about my boss's turn of personality and reaction to my giving notice than I do about her. In fact, she had many more responses than I offered, and I did not provide a physical description of her. If a person is embedded in your setting, you are choosing to reveal that setting (city, state, country, and so forth), and you need to keep them quiet in your work to protect yourself from libel charges or to protect them from pain, then keep the writing to your internal process and out of their behavior as much as you can. Also, keep the writing to the character's actions and reveal no dialogue or identifying information whatsoever. In this situation, this boss actually screamed at me for giving notice, and there's so much more I didn't say. When it comes to memoir, it is best to reveal *your internal process* in response to actions.

Point of View

Point of view is the perspective from which you tell your story. It was popular in the eighties and early nineties to write memoir in third person, as a narrative with an objective, unknown narrator. Now, it is more popular to write it in first person, but either is acceptable. Just to make point of view clear it has to do with *person.* If you write in first person, you use the word "I" to describe yourself. If you write in third person, you use your name and "he" or "she" to describe yourself. You would *not* write memoir in second person, using "you" to describe yourself. But you might write in third person from an entirely different and creative point of view.

Jack London wrote *Call of the Wild* from the perspective of the dog in the story. Imagine for a moment writing your memoir from the perspective of your own child. You might also write from the perspective of your higher power or a wounded part of yourself or both. I will offer a writing prompt in the next section to help you get used to writing from other points of view, beyond the traditional first and third person, if you want to play around with very creative points of view. For instance, you might structure your memoir in two points of view, alternating every other chapter. Maybe you write your experience of your mother and then write the same experience from *her* perspective. If you are feeling ultra creative and are seeking a massive challenge, you could write the same experience of your memoir from the point of view of many characters. It's even possible to write your memoir from the point of view of an inanimate object, which would also be an objective narrator, in third person.

Symbolism

This is one of my favorite literary elements to teach. Most people are fifty books in one lifetime (at least, I hear fifty books in most people I meet), so they are carrying around symbols from a myriad of worlds. The best symbolism occurs without even trying. Everyone has this ability, and it's what I call the magic of creativity. You'll be writing along, not even paying much attention to trying to be symbolic, and you'll share your work with someone who notices this incredible symbolism that you didn't intend. Here's an example of a piece of mine in which I did that completely without intent.

> By early August, when my father was diagnosed with lung cancer, tar bubbled up on our country road and stuck to my shoes. It smelled like a new roof, and I could hear the bubbles pop under my feet. My thirteen-year-old sister and I were forbidden to enter the house without first removing our shoes. It was the rule of the heat. [1]

When I wrote this, I did not intend to associate tar with lung cancer, or the fact that the girls were forbidden to bring that into the

---

1   Krista Burlae. "Midwifery." *6th Annual Writer's Digest Short Short Story Competition: A Collection.* Victoria, BC: Trafford, 2006, 18.

house—just as in the rest of the story, they were forbidden to actually talk about the death of their father. Of course some symbolism is intentional and explicit, and that is fine if it is artful and not overly obvious. Weather is such a beautiful representation of emotions, and at the end of this story I intentionally set out to release the emotions of the narrator, the oldest daughter, through the weather.

> "It's going to rain," I said. "My feet are bloated." That was my telltale sign that a storm was brewing even on a cloudless day. Within an hour an arched thunderhead blew in from the west. The rain spit brutally, and steam rose from the ground, releasing the torrid force of three weeks of unyielding heat. *I want to move to Oregon*, I thought, *where it rains a lot.*[2]

You can use symbols in numerous other ways to communicate to your readers. You might choose to use the growth of a tree to symbolize your own growth, or the back-and-forth shuffle of the waves of the sea to symbolize your ambiguity. Animals, plants, landscapes, city buildings, clocks and other timepieces, phones for communication, purses for money—the list is endless. You can do an Internet search for "totem," "symbolism," or my favorite, "dream symbols," to get you thinking about how you might intentionally use symbols in your work. You might also offer a story of dropping something to symbolize dropping the ball, which brings me to another literary device that I'll briefly discuss in this section because it is also a symbol: foreshadowing.

Foreshadowing is a typically unrelated mini story that suggests something is about to occur. In my piece *Midwifery*, from which

---

2   Ibid., 20.

the quotes above are taken, the foreshadowed symbol (death) is represented below.

> My father wasn't the only one dying that summer. A seven-year-old neighbor girl was playing hide-and-seek with her brother. She hid in the trunk of her parents' Oldsmobile and locked herself inside. She won. No one found her for six hours.[3]

Foreshadowing can act as a symbol for what is to come, alerting your reader of the theme that is impending in your work; in this case, the theme was death.

The above piece is fiction. However, because memoir is art, you can offer a few artistic devices that weren't necessarily true as they happened, to beef up your story. For instance, the tree that grew in your yard and parallels your own growth may not have dropped leaves just as you dropped patterns in your life, but the use of it as a symbol is completely acceptable in memoir. However, this is not true of changing the actions of *people* in your story!

The best way to create symbolism in your work is to write. For most writers, it will just happen, which is one of those gems of the writing process that is beautiful to experience and appreciate.

---

3   Ibid., 18.

Plot

The plot of your story is the action that takes place. How you structure your story will determine how your plot unfolds. Or, if you are a writer whose story structure unfolds as you write, your plot will determine your structure. When you read, you probably don't think about plot very much, but it is what draws a reader in if handled with enthusiasm; it is the map of your book.

Consider the movie *Pulp Fiction*. The plot is not in chronological order, and when I watch that film, I always want to watch the scenes in chronological order. Quentin Tarantino was purposeful in creating a plot that is distinctly out of order, with what appears to be very little reason behind it but is likely quite artistically intentional. It appears that he starts at the end, but when you review his plot, he actually starts in the middle; further, the end of his story happens in the middle of the film. What Quentin Tarantino does with plot is very brave and unique, and for *Pulp Fiction*, it works. If you can exact a plot outside of the norm and engage your reader, then do so with pizzazz!

As you'll see in the next chapter, you can play around with plot by offering climactic events in the beginning of your work and bringing your reader up to speed in the following chapters, or by opening with the conflict and finding resolve as the story unfolds to a climax. These tactics entice the reader with a conflict that she needs to resolve, and so she keeps reading. One of the finest examples I've ever seen of this was in *The Lovely Bones* by Alice Sebold, in which the author begins the book with the murder of a child from *her* perspective. She then allows the family to break apart and heal as the result of the child's death, and she includes the child's perspective from heaven, as well as the other family members' perspectives. Retreating a moment to point of view, consider writing your memoir from the perspective of a relative who has crossed over, and then include that perspective once he or she is on the other side. Is this fiction? It really depends on what you and your readers believe!

Climax and Conflict

Every strong story has a climax, or a pinnacle point of emotional suspense for a reader. The conflict of human experience is any kind of paradox, confusion, problem, or other type of human predicament of distress you can imagine. A series of conflicts build up to this climax, and then the resolution to the conflicts arrive, perhaps in doses, until a determined ending brings the climax to a complete sense of closure (unless you plan a series of memoirs tied together by conflicting endings). You can also end your memoir with a climax if it resolves the conflict. Or, if you are capable and can end your memoir open-ended with a conflict and without planning another or a resolution, by all means do it.

You may also have a series of conflicts building upon one another, in which one or more climaxes evolve and are resolved. In Jerry Stahl's *Permanent Midnight*, he offers many climaxes in which he almost gets caught using and stealing drugs. Finally, his girlfriend confronts him for the ultimate conflict, and his resolution is to stop using drugs. The book itself is part of the cathartic transformation that Jerry makes; he needs to tell his story, just like many of us do.

To build up to climax in your memoir, you can start boldly, describing what is happening right in the beginning, or you can ease your way up to it, revealing bits and pieces until the climax is clear. Either way will likely keep your reader reading, which is your goal by offering unresolved conflicts that are uncomfortable, yet enticing enough for the reader that he keeps reading to get to a resolve. I can't imagine your need to write cathartic memoir without conflicts to resolve and climactic events!

Chapter 3: Creative Organizational Design

As I mentioned in chapter 1, you can organize your memoir in several ways, including chronological, place, character, *in medias res* or *in fine*, therapeutic, spiritual, and many others. I've been dropping all kinds of hints about ways to organize around character, point of view, and other literary elements. If you can fashion a design for yourself out of these hints, please do so! If you are looking for more structure, I'm offering it in this chapter. Or, you may use what I offer in this chapter to create your own design. By this point, you will likely be thinking a lot about how to create the map that you call the structure of your story.

Chronological

Most memoirs are arranged by chronology, or time. This is the easiest way to structure your memoir, and it's certainly a valid one. You simply start at the beginning and end at the end. Your entire story is from one point in time to another, from past to future (as it reads in the memoir, not in real life, because memoir is written in past tense about a past event in your life), but you may vacillate slightly on this.

There are several ways to structure a chronological memoir—as many ways as time is marked. You may mark time by years, but as mentioned before, life seldom happens by the calendar. You may mark time by relationships, places where you lived (which may get into place, but I'll soon offer distinctions), when you held specific jobs, when each of your children was born, and more. You may choose to demarcate time by political events, decades if it is useful, or even rings on that symbolic tree in your front yard. You may wish to talk about your story in six-month increments, and each chapter may be titled accordingly: "June 1966," "January 1967," "June 1967." But if your life events didn't happen in six-month increments, they don't have to be so measured in your writing. You could have a chapter spanning one week, and then another spanning one year. Perhaps that one week packed more than the entire next year and needs such a focus. Or, you may use seasons to mark four sections within your book, within which you choose another way to name your chapters. The seasons may even reflect your emotional content in symbol, if this was a relatively accurate reflection. Summer was a happy time; winter was a time of discontent. This doesn't mean you can't include your early childhood memories that relate to the purpose and theme of your memoir, and you can include a small section describing them in the beginning, if not an entire chapter.

In fact, if you wish to show a relationship between your childhood and your adult life, you probably should include precipitating childhood events in the first chapter. You could do so in a chronological way that then sets up the rest of the book. For instance, if the birth of your physically challenged brother created a sense of abandonment for you, and the theme of your book is about abandonment and how that affected you, then you write about that early childhood event in the beginning and set the theme for your book. If you became a caretaker and learned to ignore your own needs, and it is a theme of the memoir, include that in the initial chapter as well. Set the stage (or the page)! If you are choosing a simple, chronological structure from point A to point B and struggling to decide how to establish time, then go back to your theme and see if you can choose a time structure that relates.

Most books must use chronology in some fashion, even combined with another literary element or structure. Below is a visual example of a chronological map of a memoir.

Chronological Example

Chapter 1	Chapter 2	Chapter 3	Chapter 4	Chapter 5
Early Childhood Experiences	Time Period #1 *May, 1976: Marriage to Ken*	Time Period #2 *October, 1980: A Diary of Ken's Illness After Four Years of Decline*	Time Period #3 *Christmas 1982: Ken's Last Christmas*	Time Period #5 *June 1983: Moving On*
Author experiences the birth of a physically challenged brother.	Ken had an illness, and marrying him seemed as normal as could be.		Climax is at full force here.	Resolution: after Ken's death, the author learns to take care of self over taking care of others.
Author learns to deny her own needs to help family.		Author begins to build climax by describing the caretaking necessary for Ken's illness.	The conflict jumps to its highest climax.	
Author might have a foreshadowing experience in this chapter, beyond the early events that set up patterns and imprints in her life.	This example would likely be the beginning of the conflict created by these early patterns. The conflict will get more climatic as future chapters unfold.	The conflict grows in intensity.		

Your book may have many more than five chapters. This is just an example in visual form to show you how the map might look. You might for instance, double the number of chapters keeping the structure in place.

Place

Although I'm choosing to wait to write my memoirs at an older age for a number of personal reasons, I'm relatively certain I'll opt for some semblance of place as an organizational structure. I've moved around a lot and found that different cultures spark different experiences for me. I may not use chronology so much as shadow traits that I was able to see in various places. I've been very blessed to use my nomadic nature to find just the right experiences to bring forth a better me. The places I've lived, with their corresponding cultures, combined with events in my life have been exactly what I needed at each step of my life to get a clear view of my own shadow and how it was hurting or sabotaging me. For instance, I might choose to organize one of my memoirs around place, keeping the chronology intact from my childhood, showing the corresponding place where I was able to make that wound of my shadow visible, and addressing it with my own adult tools.

That's just one idea about how to mix time and place to organize your memoir. Maybe you need to write your memoir around places you've experienced because you've been to war. In the war hero's memoir I edited, place had a huge role in his experience because various political and war events were constantly forcing him to move country, area, and housing structure.

Furthermore, we get attached to places. Maybe you are very attached to your home, and you could, if you so choose, write your memoir in various rooms: the garden, the garage, the backyard, and other areas of your home. Maybe that expands to your city, and you want to show your experiences in varying roles through place: mother at home, teacher at work, Christian at church, drinker at the bar, whatever you are trying to present.

Finally, maybe you've spent time in other countries, and your memoir is about that experience. Maybe it makes more sense to for you to organize around each visit, rather than by chronology, or you can combine the two. It always comes back to your theme and how this organization can edify what it is you are trying to convey. How can you make your reader further understand the transformational experience that you had? How can you convey a cathartic message through your structure?

Character

I've alluded to using character to organize your memoir in both the first chapter referring to Jodi Picoult's *My Sister's Keeper* and in the second chapter under "Character and Character Building" and "Point of View." As said before, the list of ways you can organize around character is endless. One that comes to mind is to write your memoir from your perspective in one chapter, and in the next offer what might have been the perspective of your life from the point of view of a main character with whom you are involved. This character should have a strong presence in the story, and it must be useful to offer his or her perspective as it relates to your theme. As an example, perhaps you have autistic child, now an adult and you are writing about your experience of parenting this child. You might start the book with a climactic event that spurred you to write, and then you begin with what your experience was at his birth to age four. You must have enough empathy for this child by now to attempt to write what his experience was like from a cognitive point (say, age two to three) forward. Some people are even talented enough to get inside the heart of an infant and write from that perspective.

Or, maybe you write your entire memoir from the perspective of your pet, as Jack London wrote *Call of the Wild.* If you are writing about your relationship with your pet, this might be a pretty handy way to present what your pet might have felt, or what you felt about him or her. Just remember that your memoir is about *your* experience, not your pet's experience, so your pet's point of view is of *you.*

Another idea is to write memoir from varying perspectives of the characters involved. Again, it's about you, but if you feel you know them well enough, you could offer perspectives of your life from the points of view of up to about five characters, especially if they demarcate time for you. For instance, maybe you were housed with different families or foster homes as a child. You could write your memoir as perceived by those different mother figures, each offering whatever they did at different developmental stages. You could offer an adult perspective of your own in every other chapter.

You could also combine character with place. For instance, perhaps you can associate particular rooms with particular family members: mother and kitchen, father and den, brother and family room, sister and bedroom. Early in the book, you could describe each room with symbolism that matches the person with whom you associate the room. If your sister was feminine, perhaps her room had feminine items that could offer insight into her personality. Maybe your mother was known for use of particular kitchen items that represent traits that she felt.

Character/Place Combined Example

Chapter 1	Chapter 2	Chapter 3
The Family: In the Living Room	Mother: In the Kitchen	Father: In the Den
The author describes all characters and sets the stage for the story to come through foreshadowing, descriptions, innuendo, etc.	Presuming the author's mother is a main character of her memoir, the author can offer even more detail, simultaneously beginning the lead into the conflict or problem in the story.	The author can describe the den and let the contents of the den symbolize Dad's personality. The colors offer insights into his soul.
This chapter might also describe the entire house with each character's behavior symbolized by the contents of the room that the author chooses to describe. The author can align the described behavior with the physical contents of the room.		The author can choose how she describes his room, or in symbolic terms, his personality.

Obviously the above example isn't comprehensive, but you get the idea of organizing your memoir around rooms in your home and characters of your story. Change the rooms to places in your city that house specific key characters in your story if it is appropriate, or use states and countries.

Finally, you could also suggest that a particular item take the point of view, like a serving bowl. When my grandmother died, I received certain kitchen items that she'd used regularly. I've considered writing about various family meals from the point of view of her Dutch oven. The stews that simmered in that item could also be symbolic of the simmering elements and patterns of my family.

Let your creativity flourish with place, character, and point of view for your memoir structure. Only you know your theme and can apply a structure that fits. Do some free writing and see if an idea pops out for you!

In Medias Res and *In Fine*

In medias res is an old tool. You start your book in the middle of your story and then work from the beginning to the middle and then through to the end. For instance, the first chapter may be a reasonably climactic event that occurs within your story. By doing this, you start off with a mystery that will keep your reader reading to figure out how you got to this point in the first place. The second chapter then goes back to the beginning of your story, and you build up all the details that lead up to the climactic event somewhere in the middle of your book. When you actually reach the place in time in which the first chapter's event occurs, you can simply refer to it and resolve whatever suspense you created in the first and subsequent chapters. Hemmingway used this technique often and effectively.

In Medias Res

Chapter 1	**Chapter 2**	**Chapter 3**	**Chapter 4**	**Chapter 5**
The author can begin in the middle of the story at a very suspenseful part. Time Period #4 *Christmas 1982: Ken's Last Christmas* A climax is at full force here but it may not be the most climactic event in the story. The author draws the reader into the story.	The author describes the birth of her physically challenged brother. She writes about learning to deny her own needs to help family. This example would likely be the beginning of the conflict created by these early patterns. The author then builds up to the experience of chapter 1.	Time Period #1 *May, 1976: Marriage to Ken* Ken had an illness, and marrying him seemed as normal as could be. The author describes the caretaking necessary for Ken's illness. The conflict grows in intensity and may even become more climactic.	Time Period #2 *October, 1980: A Diary of Ken's Illness After Four Years of Decline* The author begins to build climax. She would offer reference to chapter 1 here and then move beyond it.	Time Period #3 *June 1983: Moving On* The author creates resolution by writing about learning to take care of self over others. She can offer examples of self-care leading to more joy.

This is just an example in visual form to show you how the map might look, but you'll likely have more.

In fine is very similar to *in medias res*; it simply means "at the end of things." You start off with a suspenseful ending and then build up to that in the following chapters.

Therapeutic

I've already discussed Jacyee Dugard's *A Stolen Life* as one example of how to write a therapeutic memoir. Like the other structures, the options are limitless as to how you write a therapeutic memoir. You might choose to put six chapters of your childhood in section 1, which corresponds with six chapters of adult life in section 2.

Two Sections with Corresponding Chapters

Section 1

Chapter 1	Chapter 2	Chapter 3	Chapter 4	Chapter 5	Chapter 6
Childhood Experience #1	Childhood Experience #2	Childhood Experience #3	Childhood Experience #4	Childhood Experience #5	Childhood Experience #6

Section 2

Chapter 7	Chapter 8	Chapter 9	Chapter 10	Chapter 11	Chapter 12
Adult experiences or patterns relating to childhood experience #1	Adult experiences or patterns relating to childhood experience #2	Adult experiences or patterns relating to childhood experience #3	Adult experiences or patterns relating to childhood experience #4	Adult experiences or patterns relating to childhood experience #5	Adult experiences or patterns relating to childhood experience #6

Chapter 1 corresponds with chapter 7; chapter 2 corresponds with chapter 8, and so on.

Or you can do this within each chapter, offering two sections in each chapter.

Two Sections within Each Chapter

Chapter 1	Chapter 2	Chapter 3	Chapter 4	Chapter 5	Chapter 6
Section 1 Childhood Experience #1	*Section 1* Childhood Experience #2	*Section 1* Childhood Experience #3	*Section 1* Childhood Experience #4	*Section 1* Childhood Experience #5	*Section 1* Childhood Experience #6
Section 2 Adult experiences or patterns relating to childhood experience #1	*Section 2* Adult experiences or patterns relating to childhood experience #2	*Section 2* Adult experiences or patterns relating to childhood experience #3	*Section 2* Adult experiences or patterns relating to childhood experience #4	*Section 2* Adult experiences or patterns relating to childhood experience #5	*Section 2* Adult experiences or patterns relating to childhood experience #6

Or you might offer the sections in every other chapter, so that odd chapters offer childhood experiences, and even chapters offer adult experiences that relate to the most immediate former chapter.

Every Other Chapter

Chapter 1	Chapter 2	Chapter 3	Chapter 4	Chapter 5	Chapter 6
Childhood Experience #1	Adult experiences or patterns relating to childhood experience #1	Childhood Experience #2	Adult experiences or patterns relating to childhood experience #2	Childhood Experience #3	Adult experiences or patterns relating to childhood experience #3

Cognitive Behavioral

Cognitive behavioral theories are theories that work with the mind for behavioral change. They are the most effective treatments for depression because they offer a schedule, if not a reward, to get people up, out, and moving—all of which is difficult when someone is depressed, and the steps are necessary to treat depression. If you had an experience in which you worked out a plan (with or without a therapist) to change your life, such as weight loss, ending an addiction, or ending depression, you used a cognitive behavioral approach. The theme of your book might be motivation.

Cognitive Behavioral Structure

Chapter 1	Chapter 2	Chapter 3	Chapter 4	Chapter 5
The habit, condition, pattern, or experience the author wants to change. She describes clearly her experience of whatever it was she changed so that the reader *feels* her pain, her prison, her need to change her life. If needed, she can offer a full or partial chapter on precipitating or childhood events that may have been part of her experience.	Crisis/Climax (possibly; maybe she changed without a crisis). The habit, condition, or pattern reaches a critical mass, or as known in AA, the author bottoms out. There is a dire need for change beyond the general discomfort of the habit or condition. The author's life, family, finances or other basic need is in jeopardy because of it.	The author's plan for change. She will likely be very specific. She can include charts and tracking tools for her changes, her fears, her belief in herself to change, her vacillation, etc.	The author's experience of change. She will show us the changes as she tracked them. She explains her emotions as she changes her patterns. She may show charts, graphs, and successes.	How has the author sustained her change? Does she feel better about the new life she has created? Is she happier? How has she changed her identity to reflect her new life?

Existential

Existential modalities, while definitely used in therapy aren't acknowledged like modalities that can be measured (such as cognitive behavioral modalities). They occur in therapeutic and other relationships all the time. Managed care will not pay for this particular type of modality because it isn't measurable. The existentialist simply exists with clients and shares in their hopes, dreams, pains, and so forth. The idea is to just be. In writing terms, I'm certain you could write about someone who existed with you through an ordeal, accomplishment, or other experience. Existentialists are in all professions and walks of life: nursing, coaching, marriages, parents, children, business partnerships and even pets. You might include chapters of what you think your experience would've been like without the people or creatures who existed around you during it. You might also write your memoir from the point of view of the person (or animal, spirit guide, or inanimate object) that existed with you through the dark period of your life.

> *How My Cat Felt When I Had to Leave Her for a Year*
> *She left me, and I can feel she's not coming back for me. My heart races when the doorbell rings, and I hope it is her, but I know it isn't. She was the best owner I've ever had, and I don't like where I am now. Children hunt me. I can't sleep in a real bed. I want my one and only owner back. It's been three full moons, and she hasn't come for me. A sadness sinks into me that I hope she feels. Does she miss me? Who knows her like I do? Does she feel alone without me? Is she going to be okay?*

What I Felt When I Had to Leave My Cat for a Year

At month three, I could feel her accept that I wasn't coming back for her; I felt a deep abandoning feeling from her. It wasn't true; it was just that I could not afford to keep her safe during that time in my life, so I left her with my mother. My gut wrenched because this cat, Shelby, was my familiar. Like witches of old, I had a guide, a friend, a bond beyond what normally occurs between animal and human, and her sadness of being left was hardly the first thing I'd felt from her. I hated leaving her but had no other choice. I could feel her grief at being abandoned, which I joined with as I missed my friend. A year later I got her back. She punished me for one day and then crawled into bed and cuddled up like we'd never been apart. She's sixteen now, and I haven't left her with anyone again, nor will I. This cat was with me during some of the worst times of my life. I'm not quite sure how it would've turned out if I'd been alone. Some relationships are just so deep, regardless of species. I'm blessed to have most all relationships like this. I'm so blessed to love so deeply.

You might wonder how animals can be so intuitive. The theme of this vignette is *intuitive* connection. This cat was able to intuit when I was ill and sit by my side, as if guarding me, only leaving me to eat and use her litter box. I learned to do the same thing for her and she knew it. She trusted me with abandon and I did not breech that trust. Emotion, the language of intuition, sophisticated as it is, is very clear, very real and typically without error. The key is learning to trust it. Animals live by it. Many humans are still trying to remember how to do that. Existentialists do it naturally.

Other therapeutic modalities can offer a memoir structure for you if you would like to pursue learning about them (or already have): they include Gestalt, psychodynamic, Maslow, Rogerian, and so many more. You can also use a specific therapeutic modality to structure your memoir. Carl Jung's personality disintegration and reintegration is one option. Jung believes your overarching egos disintegrate at times in life, and it feels like your life is falling apart. Then, you restructure your ego to fit the stage of life you are in, and you are happier and healthier for the change. You organize your memoir around pre- and post-ego change. Because Jung is so much like the spiritual approaches, I'll address more of this in the following section.

Spiritual

There are many spiritual beliefs, some traditional and some innovative. If you aspire to a particular belief system or see it working in action in your life, you may wish to structure your memoir within that system. Maybe you feel challenged, like Job. Maybe you feel like you've lived through a shamanic archetype. Maybe you feel like you've experienced a dark night of the soul. Maybe you've learned dramatically from Louise Hay or Carolyn Myss.

Sacred Contracts

If you are a fan of Carolyn Myss's *Sacred Contracts: Awakening Your Divine Potential*, you might want to start your memoir having a conversation with God. Carolyn Myss is a world-renowned medical empath and author, and she suggests that our experiences on earth are contracted soulfully, before birth, and that when we encounter adversity or joy with another person, this is a contract to help promote growth. That is, before birth your soul discussed with God (or your higher power or other souls) what experiences you contract for, to learn specific lessons to allow you to complete some tasks on earth. Wayne Dyer, another inspirational author who wrote *Inspiration: Your Ultimate Calling*, went so far as to suggest his own conversation with God based on his self-reported soul contract to inspire people and heal (which he does). Some of my earlier work focuses on issues of socioeconomic class and poverty as an experience of violence. If I were to guess what my conversation with God was, it would go something like this:

> ME: *God, I want to go to earth to learn how help the poor in hierarchical nations. I hope to write a book about how poverty and violence are intertwined. What do you think my life would look like?*
>
> GOD: *How about a single-parent household in rural Indiana with a family who doesn't see the value of your desire for education or artistic endeavor? You will be given a very sensitive body and heart of an artist, and you'll be asked to do things against your nature much of your early life, in order to survive. It will feel violent to you, so you can experience this combination personally. You'll find a way to educate yourself, travel frequently, become a writer, and present what you've learned to the world.*
>
> ME: *Wow, sounds like I'll learn a lot from that. Let's do it.*

I've often asked my soul (especially when I was homeless), "Soul, what were you thinking when you made that contract?" Of great fortune in my life, I've honored the contract and subsequent book, and I have moved into a different way of life, complete with its own contracts and experiences.

This is another favorite section of mine to write and teach because it is so fascinating to understand these authors. They've helped me in so many parts of my life that I can't begin to consider writing memoirs without referring to them. One tiny piece of my memoir that I'll reveal now to capture a soul contract follows.

In 2006 I was wandering. I'd just left my last job as a therapist through a divine call, and I was ready to leave the field. That job was working in a high-security, residential agency with juvenile sex offenders, and it was tough. I had very little money to my name, about $12,000, but I know to listen to divine calls, so I left the job and did my best to trust that all would be well. I lived in Northern California, up in the rural country just south of Oregon, and I needed water to help me to decide what to do, so I drove west until I heard the splash of the Pacific. While there, I got a really clear call to go to Seattle and present some academic work at the University of Washington. I'd tried to present my pioneering work to the university before, and no one responded. Under a redwood, I heard clearly to try again. I went home from my week-long excursion of sleeping in my SUV along the coast, called UW, and got right in for a presentation. I made a reservation for a decent hotel in the U district of Seattle. I bought a flight.

I did not get anywhere with my presentation, except to learn I had a lot of work to do that I could not afford to do. But the divine knew I would follow up with my creative work, and so it called me through that. However, while in Seattle three things happened. One, I signed a lease, hoping to move there and find work, but even before 2008, that was a sketchy plan at best. Seattle, like Portland, had a lot of jobs that don't support the standard of living and post-2008 crash those were fewer and farther between. Two, I got a job interview in Napa, California, for a half-time position doing mediations with the court there—also a sketchy arrangement to try to support myself on half of an income. Three, I met a man, Charles, at the hotel, at the restaurants nearby, and on the streets of Seattle over and over again, with whom I formed an acquaintance that week. It turns out Charles, whom I met randomly in this city of five million people, was from Bisbee, Arizona, the town where I was homeless and had left just eight months earlier. Charles and I had so many connections between us that it was truly unreal. I returned to California, and we talked by phone for about four weeks.

One Friday morning I received a divine call to move to Nebraska (where Charles then resided). I fought it. I'd clawed my poverty-ridden butt out of the Midwest and could not for the life of me understand why I should return there. I was contemplating this divine call, wondering if I was nuts, and as I often do during times of change, I went to church. Usually when I go to church, I miss the entire sermon because God speaks to me directly—screams actually. This time I got: "Teach writing." In one of my many negotiations with God, I said, "Show me the way. I have no idea how to start doing this, with now only $9,000 to my name!" And God did.

As I went home from church, I found a random tape that I thought would be unfamiliar music that I could enjoy. I popped it in the tape deck of my dilapidated SUV, and it was Carolyn Myss's voice ringing out: "And if your angel tells you to move to West Virginia and you don't listen, it could be *five more years until you hear from your angel again." I went home, called Charles, and asked him if he'd help me make the transition to Nebraska. Strangely, after knowing me for just about four weeks in Seattle and by phone, he agreed. And so I sold all of my things, packed the cat on the console, and drove east to the heart of the country, where I not only taught writing but edited exciting memoirs; met wonderful people; healed old, harsh wounds; and found my calling. I grew so much there, that I can only understand these calls as exactly what I needed. I am so grateful now that I listened to my intuition!*

I've always felt that Charles and I had a sacred contract to fulfill by coming together.

Dark Night of the Soul

Many people experience a dark night of the soul as defined by St. John of the Cross. In a nutshell, he revealed the following insights:

1. People who are on a path to enlightenment experience a long and enduring period of difficulty.

2. During this period they are seeking externally what can only be found internally: their inner voice to God. They seek and seek, and they never find.

3. Just when they think they can't bear another year, month, or day of their difficulty, they experience it *en masse*. It's like all their personal difficulties are magnified and concentrated into one or two years. Some people live through it, and some do not.

4. If they live through it, they achieve connection with God and enlightenment—which is not to say that life is perfect, but merely softer to experience and far more joyful. If they don't live through it, they achieve enlightenment in another way. [4]

If you've experienced a dark night of the soul, the difficulties described in the third item are a possible climax of your story. If you structure your story around the dark night of the soul, you would have the following structure.

Dark Night of the Soul Structure

First Several Chapters	Central Chapters Climax:	Final Chapters
How you, prior to your dark night, needed to find your higher power outside of your own heart.	These chapters are a clear description of the event or events in your life that constitute your dark night of the soul.	These chapters include your experience of life after your dark night of the soul.
Include how seeking to ameliorate your pain externally seemingly created more.	You offer how your issues came to a culmination and were nearly intolerable, if not near death.	You include descriptions of your internal connection with your higher power instead of seeking it through external, earthly sources as in the early chapters.
These chapters are about how you created more pain for yourself in not understanding your internal, spiritual self.		

---

4   Paul Negri and T.N.I. Rogers, eds. *Dark Night of the Soul*. Translated by E. Allison Peers. Grand Rapids: Christian Classics Ethereal Library, 2003.

Other Spiritual Perspectives

If you are a fan of Don Miguel Ángel Ruiz's *The Four Agreements*, you might structure in two halves. One half is the poison you received from your upbringing and the culture at large, the other your cathartic transformation in making new, more empowering, and loving agreements with the world. You might also structure the memoir to represent this in every other chapter. I've met numerologists who'd rather die than not use their numerology to support their work. If you are a three, maybe every third chapter is about the transformative aspects of your new agreements, and the other two are about your poison. You could even offer thirty chapters, keeping the symbolism of your work in your book!

In Debbie Ford's book *The Dark Side of the Light Chasers*, she suggests that every criticism you have of other people is actually a criticism you feel about yourself. Further, she suggests that for each criticism you feel, there is a corresponding light side that you can access. For instance, if people who are very analytical bother you, it is likely that this part of yourself is one you haven't forgiven. The corresponding light side of this would be to be very compassionate and loving, first toward yourself, and then you will find that it resonates outward to others.

You could organize your memoir in this fashion, especially one around transformation from dark to light. You could talk about the judgment to which you hold tight, the button that gets pushed in you by other people, and how you internally altered it by using love and compassion toward yourself for being human. Your organization would include sections in both shadow and light, describing how your external world changed as you changed your perception of what is happening around you. Again, you could organize in two large halves, or in a varying chapter-by-chapter fashion.

There are so many spiritual beliefs upon which you might reflect and offer a structure for your memoir. If I haven't mentioned your favorite one thus far, then fashion one you can use based upon your own belief system!

Your Personal Imprint

Maybe you've lived long enough—or hard enough, light enough, or just enough—to develop your own way of seeing the world. Perhaps you no longer seek out spiritual information through others, because you've found it within your own heart. For instance, I see that people have an imprint that they share with the world; it has both dark and light qualities. They walk about the world reflecting this everywhere they go. An example that comes to mind is a man I once knew who was nearly a hoarder. He kept several of everything around and was very attached to his stuff. He was equally attached to the people in his life, even if he was not particularly close to them. He was a rock for a lot of people because he could attach to so many at once and maintain a reasonably good relationship with all of them. His attachment to stuff seemed to parallel his attachment to people. He eventually changed his lifestyle so that he was less attached to people he didn't care deeply for, and he simultaneously rid himself of several things in his life. One of my worldviews is that people act out in their homes what they act out in the world around them. I could easily write with the symbolism of what is in one's home and extrapolate out into the world in which they interact. Perhaps you have a worldview as well. If so, feel free to create your own memoir structure out of your own way of seeing the world, yourself, and others within it.

Chapter 4: Angel Assignments

"Angel Assignments" is a phrase I'm using to describe things you can do to jumpstart your writing throughout this process. In this section, I'll offer you lots of tools to get you started and keep you going; they include necessary distraction, quieting the analytical mind, brainstorming, earthy tricks, exercise options, and your initial audience. Refer to this section as often as you like and use the prompts as you write. Feel free to e-mail any new variations to us![5] You'd be surprised how such simple things can keep your creativity moving and flowing.

For a writer, one of the hardest things to do is to start each time she sits down to write. But what really separates a writer from everyone else is that *she writes*. It is not uncommon to sit at the computer for ten minutes and write nothing. Think about this: for most of your life, you've had a parent, teacher, or boss define exactly what you should do and how you should do it. Now, it's just you and God (or your higher power), and you have to completely be that authority who defines what you do, when you do it, and how. That is a very difficult thing to do. Furthermore, becoming your own authority is

5   info@catharisjournal.com

very freeing: for once in your life you are doing something without that financial or emotional prodding—you are the authority of your own work of art; *you are the author!* The first three tools I offer help you get started; the others help you in the middle when you feel blocked. Please use them as they work for you and mix them with your own. Upgrade them for yourself. Your story is important, or you wouldn't have purchased this book and all the implements, much less read this far.

I suggest you use a pen or pencil and journal for many of the exercises. Most people learned to write originally with a pen or pencil and the creative mind is different when we use tools that are closer to the earth and our earliest memories—especially in memoir. In my own writing, I can write publishable work quickly with a pen or pencil (my earliest tool). When I try it on the computer, it's as if my natural creativity is somehow thwarted compared to the pen and paper. If you feel that the computer works better for you, then by all means use it, but you might try both and see what is best for you to get your creativity flowing.

Necessary Distraction

When I wrote my first book, my apartment was clean on the days I wrote. I was worthless without coffee in the morning, and I had to check my e-mail to make sure nothing emergent was taking place to keep me from writing, which the trickster in me *really wanted.* You are most likely going to try to keep yourself from writing by such distractions, so I suggest building them into your writing time. Just let yourself lose focus if you need to, but limit it to five minutes or fewer. Whatever it is you do to distract, plan for it in your writing time. You have to clean anyway, so clean the day before you write. Be very wary of ingesting chemicals, including sugar beyond a healthy amount. If you like to eat when you write, put cauliflower or celery on your desk. Have a glass of water available (far from your computer).

If you are struggling with the week or month that you start writing in addition to the day or hour, I highly recommend Stephen Pressfield's book *The War of Art: Break Through the Blocks and Win Your Inner Creative Battles*. He makes us all feel like we are normal in distracting ourselves, if not driving ourselves crazy, trying to avoid writing or other artistic projects. It's just the way it is. You have your angel and your trickster on each shoulder, and one of them wins. Find ways to make it your angel.

Finally, if you are bogged down with emotions and details from your daily life, Julia Cameron suggests in her book *The Artist's Way* that you should write three pages each morning (known as morning pages) about whatever is going on in your life, just to clear it from your writing; then you can start working on your book. I've known many writers who use this technique as a necessary tool that rids them of emotional distraction, and it is very effective.

Exercise

Directory of Distractions

In the chart below, list all the possible distractions you do or might do before writing on the left side. On the right side of the chart, put a time limit on this distraction, a separate time that you achieve this task (such as cleaning your home the day before you write), or a solution such as "morning pages." List more than one solution for each trickster that trips you up. Have your arsenal ready!

Your Trickster	*Your Angel*

Quieting the Analytical Mind

Editors have great analytical minds for offering critical feedback to writers. We all have an internal editorial critic that is very analytical. For people steeped in academia or other logic-heavy professions, that part of the mind takes over as a default. Many writers have difficulty shifting into more creative writing after years of learning to bow to the higher mind. In fact, academia tends to make idiots of writers: it constantly suggests that an author should defer to others and cite their work (who've deferred to others and cited their work, who've deferred to others …). Yet the term "author," from which the word "authority" is derived, is just that: one who is knowledgeable in the subject matter of her writing, who takes authority, and who offers clear and insightful commentary *from her own mind*—not that of her predecessors for their own sake and name on a page. Most certainly you are the best authority of your own life, so start believing that you are an author. If you struggle with this, try the following exercise.

This exercise puts so much pressure on the analytical mind that it can't help but defer to the creative part of you for answers. Our creativity and intuitive center lie in the occipital lobe of the brain, along with body temperature regulation, breathing, and heart rate. That is how natural it is to be creative. The analytical mind, requiring many more steps to an artless outcome, simply doesn't have time to make all this happen in ten minutes. You may not write anything to do with your memoir, but you can find your creative voice again.

Exercise

End Editing, Annihilate Analysis

Materials needed: timer, journal, pen or pencil.

Step 1: Alphabetize the following list in your journal:

forehead
smiled
closed
helped
jumped
headache
hospital
lollipop
question
railroad
remember
sandwich
scissors
shoulder
tomorrow
upstairs
vacation
restroom

Step 2: Set your timer and write for ten minutes (and only ten minutes) using the alphabetized list on the right side. Keep the words in the order you just placed them as you write. Stop after ten minutes—no cheating!

Once you truly believe you are the author of your own story, and you've distracted your analytical mind enough to find your creativity again, go ahead and write. When you stop to go back and criticize what you just wrote, *stop yourself.* You can edit anytime or hire someone. For now, just write and get the story out. Don't censor or worry about how it will read. If you still can't do it without stopping yourself, do this exercise again, alphabetizing by the second letter (or make your own word list). You can generate word lists online by typing "generate word lists" into a search engine and following the bouncing ball.

Brainstorming

This section is really helpful for the writer who organizes structure independently while writing. The act of brainstorming opens up ideas that are otherwise hidden and not available to the conscious mind. It can get you writing when you are blocked, or it can get you started when you are distracted. When you brainstorm, you have absolutely no structure or very little; you just let the words fly out of your mind through your pen, without concern for the structure of grammar, sentences, paragraphs, or anything but free flow.

Brainstorming is to get you thinking creatively and not analytically about your subject. When you think analytically, you line things up in your mind, question your process, and can easily slip into page fright in getting your story on the page. When you brainstorm, you have no concern for what you are writing.

Exercise

Setting

Materials needed: timer, journal, pen or pencil.

Brainstorming Time: This is a fun exercise. Simply choose the year you intend to write about (and it will likely be more than one), and write down every cultural event you can think of to edify your story. You can include political events, styles (anyone remember neon shoelaces?), music, acts of mass violence—whatever *you* remember if you lived in that time. Set a timer and do this for ten to twenty minutes. If you find you didn't get enough, by all means use the Internet to enhance this exercise. You will find yourself bouncing around the year in ways you'd forgotten.

You can also brainstorm your personal events for that year. As you move through your creativity, you'll remember more and more from your life that you'd tucked away somewhere in your mind. You may or may not use pieces from this list or the one above, but you'll have a full arsenal of reference material for that time to make your memoir seem very real to your reader! We all love to be reminded of humorous clichés that tie into our personal lives from the past.

Brainstorming Place: Like time, you can also brainstorm all the places that might be part of your story. If you recall them all, you can then add descriptions of them. Allow your mind to focus on place, and let your pen roll.

Characters

Every memoir has characters, because every life has a cast of people who set the relational stage for our dramas and soulful contracts. When considering what characters you are going to include, consider two very important things: (1) How do they relate to your theme? (2) Can you describe them purposefully, without judgment?

Your book has different sections, with different places and times, so you may have quite a few characters. In a memoir, you want to focus on that event or purpose you are compelled to write about, so your main characters will fall in that timeframe and place. Other less important aspects of setting will include characters, but keep it as simple as you can. Remember to include characters that relate to your theme.

Brainstorming Characters

On the following pages, use the provided charts to describe your characters. The first chart is for your main section of your memoir—the one that describes your purpose or defining events. In describing your characters, be sure to offer descriptors that can be used to regularly identify the character. For example, if your mother smoked and coughed a lot, include that to make her come to life in her character. Also, as the chart suggests, offer some dialogue that was common for the person.

Brainstorming Characters

Character	**Descriptors**	**Common Dialogue**
Grandpa Joe	*Gruff, tall, always in overalls, had a belly, waddled, often sat at dining room table and tapped his fingers on the table. Had a flat-top buzz of white hair.*	*Dirty little rip; Out yon; You sure are an odd bird; Why aren't you married yet? I only paid $X for that!*

You may not use all of the characters you come up with on this page. Use those that are most relevant to the story. Readers can only attach to about five characters in a given section. You can include others, but be very careful as to *why* you choose to include a character. Building characters is a lot of work in your writing, and you want to offer strong characters that are relevant to your story. Less strong ones are ancillary. Use the chart above to begin developing characters in your story.

Brainstorming from Various Points of View

In the following exercise, write three paragraphs in your journal about the most climactic experience of your memoir, from one or more of the following points of view. Write for twenty to thirty minutes on each.

1. A main character as strong as yourself in the story

2. An inanimate object that is consistent in your life

3. A person who has crossed over and who would know your story and internal process

Theme

In each person's life story, and in each memoir, there is a theme (or more than one). Theme is the general message of a book, and in the case of a cathartic memoir, it is also one's life purpose. The theme of your memoir is the implied view of life and your conduct, as well as the impressions within it. Your story reveals how you view the world and a suggested purpose of your life. An example might be, "I was born to help people understand their higher calling." From there, you'd express your life story in a way that leads to that understanding of your role in this world.

Theme can also include phrase generalizations like hope, faith, courage, overcoming adversity, helping the poor, or assisting those who are dying. In cathartic memoir you explore how your life experiences and individual traits, traumatic and otherwise, have shaped your personality to be the very perfect *you* that allows you to complete the tasks of your life purpose. Below are five questions to help you develop your sense of purpose and theme in writing this book. On the fifth question, you should be able to offer three generalized phrases or sentences that constitute the theme of your book.

1. If you had to summarize your reason for being on earth (and writing this book) into three single words, what would they be?

    Example: *teaching, writing, love*

2. Your reason for being on earth may or may not be a career choice. It may be to love a disabled child in your life, to help your father die, or some other purpose that only *you* know about. Your early childhood experiences will likely reflect an ability to know compassion for your purpose. In one sentence, and not using the words in question number one, describe your purpose.

    Example: *I am here to assist people in expressing their life stories.*

3. If you know about your mother's pregnancy with you, your birth story, or any of your baby months or years, describe them here. If you can ask her or another family member about it, do so. Write about your birth if you know about it, here.

Example: *From week two through week four of my life, I went hungry and lost weight. I was also born late (and have had many achievements in my life, but usually later than other people achieve them).*

4. Describe your earliest memory of a profound childhood experience that helped you to be the person with your life purpose.

Example: *When I was nine years old, I wrote a poem for school that the teacher argued I'd stolen from a Hallmark card. I did not, but I remember feeling respected by the fact that she thought I could write like a Hallmark card—and simultaneously hurt that she assumed I'd lied. The theme here is the experience of feeling emotional paradox, one that would be with me (and everyone) profoundly for a lifetime.*

5. Offer three to five sentences that you believe are the theme of your book.

Example: *I am a teacher and writer. I help people write books that express a purpose-driven life of adversity turned to triumph. I've experienced many adversities and triumphed over them, offering me the compassionate view of others who have harsh experiences. I also help people turn fear into love.*

Other Disciplines

Just when you think you can't write another word, you may stop and turn on your favorite music. You get lost in it for a bit and then easily return to your writing to finish the chapter. You can use other creative disciplines to remove writers' block, and it can work wonders when you need it. Whenever I listen to Sarah McLachlan, I go right into analytical writing. Her music was very popular when I was in graduate school and writing paper after paper. For creative writing, I tend to listen to music without words.

You could also visit a nearby art museum, read a genre outside of what you are writing, or carry out some other form of intellectual or creative pursuit. For instance, you could work on a crossword puzzle, work out a math problem by hand, or cook a meal. All creative endeavors can help refocus your mind.

You could paint, make music of some sort, or work on a craft of your choosing. Painting, like writing, can be completed in a short period of time, or it may take several months if the piece is complicated and intricate, like your memoir. On the other hand, music is quite in the moment, and if you aren't composing, you can shift your block through singing, playing an instrument, or listening to music you love. If it is a craft you enjoy, let it open your mind and alter your writing to whatever it is you need. Whatever you do, put a time limit on it.

Earthy Tricks and Exercise Options

I cannot tell you how many times nature has opened my mind to the optimum writing experience. When blocked, I will often take a walk, put my hands in dirt of some sort to connect with the earth, or stand in a warm rain storm and allow the experience to remind me of why I'm here. I once knew a writer who made snow angels when she was blocked.

Some people connect with trees, ocean, mountains, or even grass. Whatever feeds your spirit, bring it into your writing life and commune with it as you write. If you are a city person, take the bus, train, or another mode of transport to get yourself out of a block. Let your passions be your angel who knocks the trickster aside and opens your heart and mind to writing the right passage on each and every page. Incorporate what you love of earth and city into your writing routine.

Earthy tricks don't require trips to the city and countryside—you can do all kinds of things in and around your home that connect you to the earth such as cooking, gardening, growing plants, drying herbs, chopping wood, and a personal favorite of mine: chopping vegetables while listening to my favorite music. The smells and sounds seem to open a creative door each and every time I do this! You can access the *New York Times, The New Yorker, The Atlantic* or any other periodical or book with which you resonate. Let urban voices come to you. Just be sure to keep writing your voice distinct from that of any author you may be reading at the time.

Exercise is a must with most all creative projects. You are far more likely to create with authenticity if your body is in good working order than if it is not. I once encountered a yoga student who stated that his piano playing became far more creative as he found solace in his yoga practice. Runners, walkers, yogis, and swimmers all need their natural fix to work. If you don't have such a fix, consider bringing one into your writing life.

Your Initial Audience

If you are lucky, you have a support system available to you when you write. Maybe you have an editor, writing group, or partner, which I'll discuss in the next chapter. However, lives are busy, and asking someone to read everything you write may not be a possibility. Therefore it is essential to *assume* an audience as you write, perhaps even if you do have the support of others.

You should consider two types of audiences. The first is the earthly audience to whom you hope to market your book. Any editor at a publishing house would ask you to consider your audience, and if you are self-publishing, you will also have to consider who your market is. Obviously memoir can take on many audiences. I think of Mitch Albom's *Tuesdays with Morrie: An Old Man, a Young Man, and Life's Greatest Lesson,* which circulated the globe and captured six million readers. There are no-holds-barred on the types of readers who may be interested in cathartic memoir; people want to feel inspired. Yet if you are considering a general trade market (the general population), you must consider an initial marketing plan to reveal your work and choose the audience you hope to reach: men, women, teenagers, older adults, baby boomers, or someone else. Perhaps your memoir is about your experience of giving birth under bizarre circumstances; you are then most likely writing to women. As you write, imagine them reading your work and how they might benefit from it. As it occurs to you, write down places you can reach these women—for example Internet groups, hospitals, and midwifery communities. You will be using these venues later to market your book. Imagine your typical reader as someone with whom you are having a conversation, and allow that to help you continue writing. This reader needs what you have to say, or you wouldn't be bothering with all of this work.

The second type of audience you need to consider to help you stay with your project is someone who is or was close to you. Perhaps this person is alive and in your presence and is a true supporter of your happiness in this world. Whether or not she is available to read your work as you write, you know she loves you and has your best interests at heart. Write to her as if you are telling her your story. Or perhaps this person has crossed over, and your memory of him is similar: loving, supportive, wanting happiness for you. Place a picture of this person on your desk and have that conversation with him each time you write. Finally, you can even extend this to your ancestors. Most likely what you are writing about has some root in your early, if not ancestral, family history, and these souls are rooting for you. Picture them and write to them. Don't let them down! You have no idea the karmic healing that may take place because you are writing your story.

Chapter 5: Workshopping and Editing

Writers in process need both workshopping and editing most of the time. Of course there are the rare ones who can write a book that needs very little workshopping or editing, but most of us need some help. I'll distinguish between the two. Workshopping is having others read your work, or you reading aloud it to others for feedback. It can take the form of a writing partner or writing group. Editing is when someone reviews your book, usually by reading it two or three times over to find grammar errors, issues with sentence structure, typical synonym errors, and a host of other things that I'll offer in an editing checklist later in the chapter.

Workshopping

The feedback of workshopping is usually artistic in nature: good metaphor, you lost your plot structure on page 29, your tertiary character disappeared after chapter 2, excellent description, etc. Workshopping gives you a chance to see how readers will react to your work. I like it best when I read aloud, because it gives me a chance to hear my own work instead of reading it on the page it over and over. The format of presentation is your choice or that of your group.

Knowing When You Are Ready for Workshopping

Knowing when you are ready for workshopping is very clear. If you want to change nothing at all, you are probably not ready to hear healthy critique from your partner or group. The nice thing is that *you* get to decide when you are ready for workshopping. You'll know by checking at least three of the possible responses below when someone offers you feedback.

____ "Yes, I do need to change that."

____ "Thank you for noticing. It was purposeful, and I will keep it that way." (You may not even need to mention anything here; just know it internally and thank your critic.)

____ "Thank you, I'll consider that."

____ You are calm in hearing the feedback, not defensive but ready to listen.

If you find yourself fighting the criticism, one of two things is happening. One, you really aren't ready to hear feedback on your work. Don't worry; some time away from it will help that along, and you'll know because you won't feel so attached to your work. The other possibility is that you've asked the wrong person to look at your work.

Finding the Right People

Finding the right group or partner is vital to your success. First of all, you want a group or person who is close to your skill level. If you choose someone whose skills are beyond yours, you might feel frustrated, like you can't keep up. You'll get this from an editor anyway, so for workshopping, choose people who can relate to where you are. If you choose people beneath your skill level, you may be working much harder than your group or partner. If you don't find the right partner or group, don't give up and remember that the universe provides exactly what you need at just the right time. The perfect arrangement will arrive for your project. For Zora Neal Hurston, that perfect arrangement was posthumously. Although that may be disturbing to you now, it may be the case for you that your work is beyond the present day, or your perfect arrangement happens in ten years, not in ten weeks. The rule to follow is this: if you are trying to get water out of a dry well, look elsewhere. In other words, if you spend months trying to find the right writing partner or group, and it doesn't arrive, shift your focus onto something else for a while and see if the universe allows you to happen upon it serendipitously. See the checklist below for choosing people with whom you can workshop. You will need to fill it out for yourself first and then find people who match. To match, you each need to have a similar background, or a similar number of items on the checklist. For instance, you would not want to work with a book-published author as an equal if you have checked "none of the above." But you might take a workshop from a book published author who leads you through the process. Or, you might work with someone who has taught English, while you have acted as an editor.

____ Author has prior publications in the form of articles, short stories, or essays.

____ Author is book published.

____ Author is or has been an editor.

____ Author has taught English, creative writing, or another writing course.

____ Author has an MFA or another advanced degree in writing.

____ Author has other skills in writing and editing not mentioned here.

____ Author has none of the above.

Just a note: always read a few chapters of someone's work before you decide to make a commitment. You can decide by how the work is as to whether you can follow through with a long-term commitment of reading and workshopping with her regularly. Your partner or group members need to be reasonably coherent in their writing for you to offer them clear assistance. As an editor, I've recommended clients seek out a creative writing course if their skills weren't strong enough to sustain my feedback. You can discern in the same way and say no if you don't think you are up to the task of workshopping a memoir that isn't clear and coherent. Below is a checklist to contemplate when considering a group or partner.

____ The writing has reasonable amount of proper grammar and punctuation, so that it is readable.

____ The writing engages you enough to continue reading. (This may not be the author's skill level but your interest level. Either way, it is important that you are interested enough in the topic to help your partner or group by reading thoroughly.)

____ The writing is organized enough that you won't have to act as writing teacher from the get go.

____ The writing is clear and coherent enough for you to comment or react emotionally.

_____ The author seems motivated to finish with you.

_____ The author is kind in all sorts of responses and includes positive ones to keep you going.

(This one is really important, or you may lose steam.)

Rules and Etiquette for Workshopping Groups

Every writing group has to start somewhere. If you join an existing one, you will have to acclimate to the rules they have already established. You might initially ask for some of the rules below until you feel emotionally safe and comfortable with the group's process. If you can create a group of your own, I recommend using the ground rules below to get it started. Creating a group allows you to start with people all in the same place as you.

You may want to workshop your memoir as you write, or after you've completed the manuscript. It depends on what you need from the group or partner. While writing this workbook, I met with a partner periodically to keep me focused, and I completed it in the fall and winter of 2012. I needed the motivation of meeting with someone who was going to read my work. We were a good match in that we'd both edited several manuscripts. She offered editing skills that I didn't specialize in, and I offered her the same. We decided to work together, and our partnership was successful. But when I wrote my first book, I could not find a writing group, and I waited several years until I found an editor that could help me with it. I offered her the completed manuscript, and I rewrote it free of the attachment I'd felt toward it four years earlier, when I'd originally written it. If what you want is motivation, use your group or partner for this purpose as well as getting feedback on your work. If what you want is simply feedback, then complete your manuscript first. It doesn't matter if other members want motivation and you don't; as long as you show up with a chapter to workshop, you'll have something to offer the partner or group.

Rules

1. In the first four weeks, only offer positive remarks but keep track of things the author may want to know later, after trust is established.

2. Refrain from negatively commenting on content, especially in cathartic memoir. Members may write of spiritual experiences in which others do not believe. Workshopping is not a place for debate.

3. Refrain from commenting on content much at all. The group is about readers' (or listeners') reaction to the presentation of a story. In *Gerald's Game,* Stephen King wrote 352 pages on a woman handcuffed to a bed and how she lives through the ordeal and gets out of it. One wouldn't think that's particularly interesting, but his *presentation* keeps readers hooked like gawkers at a train wreck. The only time you might offer feedback on content is if you think what someone is writing might hurt the author or another person in some way.

4. Throughout the group's duration, offer 50 percent more positive than negative remarks. Remember, some people are there for motivation. The editor can be the bad guy.

Editing

Unlike workshopping, editing is a much more thorough critique of your work. It is very hard to edit your own work, and editing should be completed by someone you trust to be both honest and kind enough in the critique to keep you engaged in the project. There are essentially two different kinds of editing. One is developmental editing and the other is copyediting. Developmental editing looks for consistent connection to theme, appropriate description of setting (or lack thereof), strong character development and good use of characters, consistent and suitable use of point of view, believable symbolism, logic in your plot structure that readers can follow, intensifying conflict with a plausible climax and resolution, consistency in style, and the ability to show instead of tell.

Copyediting is looking for grammatical errors; various forms of consistency within your given style guidelines (for memoir, the *Chicago Manual of Style* is one of the most common and accepted style guidelines); common writing errors such as using the wrong word (e.g., to, too, and two); consistency in personal writing style; run-on sentences; comma, colon, and semicolon errors; sentence fragments; comma splices; verb tense; and so much more, which will be identified in the copyediting checklist.

Knowing You're Ready for Editing

Like workshopping, authors have to feel comfortable and ready for editing to be effective. Unlike workshopping, editing is far more critical. A good editor will understand the Pavlovian response of a writer needing to hear a positive remark every so many pages. Below is a checklist of items to help you determine whether you are ready for editing. You need to meet at least the first three items on this list to be ready for an editor. If you meet the last two as well, you are quite ready for editing.

_____ Author can hear criticism about mistakes (mostly) for her own benefit.

_____ Author is prepared to rewrite several passages of the memoir, which may take as long as writing the original draft.

_____ Author has a good feeling about the editor with whom she is working.

_____ Author can, when appropriate, argue a legitimate point about not making a change in her work.

_____ Author is confident to not even argue her point, but simply leaves a particular passage as it is because it is as she pleases— but it must make sense and be accurate.

Developmental Editing Checklist

An outside editor that you identify as competent should complete the following sections for you (and anything he or she sees fit). Like writing groups and partners, editors should have some track record of work for you to review. If you don't have access to such an editor for your first editorial review, consider the most detailed person you know and offer them the two editing checklists in this book from which to work. You can also decide whether or not your writing partner or one of group members could act as an editor for you.

Of course your editor will comment within your manuscript, either electronically or with a pen if you offer a hard copy. But he may use the allotted spaces below for additional commentary.

____ **Consistent Connection to Theme:** The author has chosen one, two, or perhaps three themes that represent her work. Nearly all passages in a memoir should relate back to that theme. Sometimes an editor will notice entire passages or even chapters that rabbit trail, or take a completely different direction and thus alter the theme. Unfortunately, even if they are well written, the editor should suggest cutting those passages because it can make a memoir feel incoherent. Use the space below to comment on the author's ability to stay consistent with his or her theme.

____ Appropriate Description of Setting: Ideally, setting will change throughout a memoir, and therefore the author will describe time and place again and again, if necessary. One author I worked with described time and place at the beginning of each chapter. It could also be every third or fourth chapter, or whenever setting changes. Editors can look for rich descriptions in time and place that allow the reader to be transported to that setting. I once edited a war memoir that was so rich in description that at times I felt I was in 1939 during the occupation of Warsaw. The author was excellent at showing a scene through rich, descriptive words; it was like painting a picture. As Joseph Zygielbaum notes on page 20 of *The Odyssey of a Partisan: A Memoir,*

> It was a day typical of warm Southern California. The hot breath of the Mojave Desert a hundred miles away had already overpowered the cool breezes blowing in from the Pacific. Heat waves, generated by the warm sands rose like transparent serpents into the white-flecked sky. The San Gabriel Mountains sloped into the foothills so gently that ridges and gullies resembled the folds of a great brown blanket.[6]

Further, as mentioned earlier, perhaps you are masking information by reducing the amount of description in your setting. If that is the case, the editor should be able to tell you if you have been effective in both telling your story and masking the information you wish to keep private.

6   Joseph L. Zygielbaum. *The Odyssey of a Partisan: A Memoir.* Lincoln, NE: Arthur Zygielbaum, 2009, 20.

Your editor can use the space below for comments on appropriate description of setting throughout your book depending on your intention.

____ Strong Character Development and Good Use of Characters: Every character you use needs to have at least two basic elements: (1) she is a necessary part of your story; (2) she is recognizable in her choice of words, consistent mannerisms, and emotional experience you convey of her. The more important the character to your story, the more a reader should be able to attach to or experience her. Readers may also be so disturbed they can't attach to the character (as may have been your experience). An editor should feel this, too, in the way you describe your character. If the character development was intentionally set so that you represent a person who is hard to attach to authentically, then you've done your job. It is all a matter of intention. An editor should ask you if it is your intention to create what he or she feels of your character, to make sure that feeling and intention are congruent.

Again, see Zygielbaum's description of his main character (written in third person in the '90s).

> Kuba Mordecai's face was that of a mild man. His dark hair was not as thick as it once was when it blew wildly in the biting wind of western Russia. His slight stature belied his actual capacity for dragging a machine gun through the mud of a Polesye swamp. His hands were those of a sensitive and educated man, but they also had held the gun that snuffed out the life of Steinbeck. Steinbeck was the man responsible for the murders of his wife and child in faraway Poland. A small gray flecked mustache adorned Kuba's upper lip and friendly, brown eyes looked at the world with tolerance and slight weariness. [7]

---

7   Joseph L. Zygielbaum. *The Odyssey of a Partisan: A Memoir*. Lincoln, NE: Arthur Zygielbaum, 2009, 20.

Use the space below to comment generally on the writer's description of characters, use of necessary characters, and consistency in character traits.

____ Consistent and Suitable If Not Creative Use of Point of View: Earlier I offered a myriad of ways to use point of view to spice up your story, and you may do that. However, you need to be consistent regarding how you do it. If you offer your story from your point of view in chapter one and your mother's point of view in chapter two, then you need to remain consistent in this format. You might simply use your own point of view for consistency, or you might offer just one chapter of an alternate point of view. Your editor needs to make sure it works with the story. The editor can use the space below to offer comments on point of view.

___ **Believable Symbolism:** When you write, you will automatically offer some symbols in your writing, and those are often the best ones—this is what I call the magic of creativity. You are just writing, and your editor will notice you offered beautiful symbolism, and you didn't even realize you did it. You can also work at symbolism, but sometimes it sounds contrived when you work at it. Your editor should be able to distinguish that which sounds contrived and that which is believable, natural symbolism in your work. Too much symbolism will sound artificial and unnatural. An editor should feel into the symbol and notice how it affects her. If it is too obvious, then that false, manufactured feel will come through. An editor can use the space below to offer commentary on symbolism.

____ Logic in Plot Structure That Readers Can Follow: When you write your plot, whether or not you intend it, you choose a series of events that take place in the action of your story. These events need to follow a logic that allows a reader to track what is taking place. If the flow of events or action is out of logical synchronicity, then the reader can get lost. As I've discussed earlier, you can play around with sequencing by using *in medias res* or *in fine,* but however you choose to structure the plot, a reader must be drawn in and be able to continue being mesmerized by your memoir. Your editor can use the space below to comment on plot if necessary.

____ Intensifying Conflict with a Plausible Climax: The conflict is the spice of the story. In most dramas (which memoir inadvertently is), there is a problem or conflict to be resolved. It starts out small and intensifies into a climax that forces some sort of resolution. As you write, you can build the intensity of the conflict in each chapter, and the climax itself, no matter how unbelievable it may actually seem (as in a spiritual experience), can be presented in a believable fashion. Your editor needs to look for the build-up of intensity; he can do so by checking in with how he feels as he reads your work. If he is bored, he needs to tell you the intensity isn't building. He might also feel overwrought, in which case the intensity is too high, and you'll need to tone it down. You can do this by offering chapters of benign description after chapters of high drama. If your climax is that you were in a car accident and visited heaven for two hours, you need to describe it in ways that allow your reader to believe it. Maybe there are cues that prove your experience, and you should include them. I once heard a woman describe seeing angels with such confidence that I completely believed her, although I've never had the experience myself. She spoke in an active voice with a passion I could not deny. You can do this in your writing as well. Your editor will feel into this just like intensity. He can offer commentary in the space below.

_____ **Consistency of Style:** Your editor needs to be cognizant of finding your style and helping you make it consistent. If you choose to describe your backyard with all the beauty of an elegant garden, then you will need to do the same for other descriptions. If you use metaphor in one chapter, you will likely need to use it in all chapters. If you use alliteration (the use of the same first letter in a series of words) in one chapter, you need to use it throughout your work. Your editor needs to look for inconsistencies in style, word choice, voice, tense, number, and so forth.

___ **Show, Don't Tell:** Most all creative work requires a lurid description of characters, setting, emotional content, and more. In many less creative genres, it is quite acceptable to say, "She was really sad." But in memoir, you could instead say, "She was hunched over, wrenched in a ball of pain. From her gut up to her throat and up and out of her mouth came a high-pitched 'Unnf.' She repeated that 'Unnf' over and over, as if releasing that pain, until she lay down and slept, eyes swollen to half-mooned slits." You can attach to that description, wrench right along with it, and feel its depth more literally than, "She was really sad."

Your editor should look for passages in which you can make readers attach through showing emotion instead of telling them how to feel. Describe the scene and trust your reader to feel it. Remember, you are the authority! Your editor can use the space below to note various passages to transfer from telling to showing.

Copyediting Checklist

____ **Spelling**: Use your computer whenever possible, but recognize that homonyms will not be accounted for with spell check (see below).

____ **It's and its:** "It's" is a contraction for the noun and verb "it is" or "it has." "Its" is possessive, meaning that it belongs to whatever "it" is.

Example: *It's* been a sunny day here in New Mexico during the monsoon season, but the rain will eventually wreak havoc on *its* opponent, the earth.

____ **Other homonyms:** rain and reign, bare and bear, there, their and they're, etc. If you aren't sure as the editor, check out the meaning of the word.

Example of misused homonyms: The bare went to the bear cupboard and couldn't find his honey.

____ **Run-on sentences:** A sentence should have one noun and one verb, unless it's complex, and then it can have more—but they must be separated by the proper grammatical device (comma, conjunction, colon, semicolon, etc.). Here are the rules:

1. If a comma separates two full sentences without a conjunction (and, but, that, whereas, etc.) the sentence is a run-on with a **comma splice**. It is actually two sentences with the wrong punctuation, or it is a complex sentence but needs that conjunction. This is a very common problem among new authors.

Example of a comma splice/run-on sentence: I was so tired, I went right to bed.

Correction #1: I was so tired. I went right to bed.

Correction #2: I was so tired that I went right to bed.

2. To avoid run-on sentences, try to limit your sentences to two nouns and two verbs at maximum. As an editor, ask the author to break down long sentences to no more than two nouns and two verbs. It is technically accurate to have more if you have the correct punctuation, but it is wordy and difficult to read without the natural pause of the period.

   Example of a run-on sentence: I was so tired I came home and went right to bed then I fell asleep for nine hours and got up the next morning to see a bird in the yard that was grabbing a worm from the soft, wet earth.

   Correction #1: I was so tired that I came home and went right to bed. Then, I fell asleep for nine hours and got up the next morning. When I looked outside, I saw a bird in the yard grabbing a worm from the soft, wet earth.

   Correction #2: I was so tired. I came home and went right to bed. Then, I fell asleep for nine hours and got up the next morning. When I looked outside, I saw a bird in the yard grabbing a worm from the soft, wet earth.

3. **Commas, colons, and semicolons:** Commas separate distinct subjects in one sentence, natural pauses, distinction of a name, and lists of nouns. Colons demarcate

lists (without verbs) after the initial noun-verb sentence. Semicolons separate two different sentences of the same subject but allow a writer to put it all into one sentence. The second clause must have something to do with the first, and it must have both a noun and a verb just like a complete sentence. The examples below show proper use of all three.

Comma: Well, my friend Jason had three children from his first marriage named Krissy, Kelly, and Bobby.

Colon: A typical Indiana summer grocery list includes the following items: ripe corn on the cob, fresh peaches, hand-churned butter, fresh tomatoes, and sweet peas.

Semicolon: It was a very stuffy and humid day; a storm blew in from the west and penetrated the heat.

____ **Sentence fragments:** These are incomplete sentences that are either lacking a noun or a verb. Note that the correction includes both a noun and a verb to complete the sentence.

Example of a sentence fragment with no verb: Grandpa's super-duper tractor in the barn.

Correction #1: Grandpa's super-duper tractor in the barn is covered under a tarp.

Correction #2: Grandpa's super-duper tractor in the barn still runs.

In the first correction, "is" is the added verb. In the second, "runs" is the added verb.

It is important to note that second person–implied sentences may not include a noun. For instance, the "you" is implied in the sentence "Go get it!" For grammatical purposes, the implied "you" is still considered a noun.

____ **Verb tense:** Memoir is written in the past, so verbs you use will be in past tense. Editors need to check that this is consistent throughout the manuscript, unless it is appropriate to use past participle (e.g., "would have been").

Example of a sentence written in present tense: Michael eats his cereal each morning with a plastic spoon.

Correction: Michael ate his cereal each morning with a plastic spoon.

____ **Verb number:** In a sentence, the noun is either singular or plural, and the verb needs to match this.

Example of a singular noun with a plural verb: There are a plethora of cockroaches in the parlor.

Correction: There is a plethora of silverware in the parlor.

____ **Fewer/less:** If you can count it, use fewer. "Less" describes mass plural nouns that can't be counted. See examples of proper use below.

There are fewer candy bars than there are cigarettes; choose your poison.

There is less poison in candy bars, but they still aren't good for you.

____ **Who and whom:** "Who" and "whom" refer to people, not things. Writers use "that'" all the time incorrectly to refer to people, when it is who or whom they need to use. Further, keeping straight when to use "who," "whoever," "whom," or "whomever" is tricky. Here are the rules.

1. "Who" is used for the subjective. If you answer the question of who with he or she, then you are using it properly. This is also true for "whoever."

    a. **Example:** *Who* fixed that grandfather clock? (She did.)

    b. **Example:** *Whoever* fixed that grandfather clock messed it up. (He did.)

2. "Whom" or "whomever" is used for the objective. Also, if you can replace whom with her or him the correct choice is whom or whomever. Finally, whomever/whoever get really tricky when the object of the preposition is implied and is really the subject (which would be "whoever"). See example (d) for this.

    a. **Example:** Maria is the person to *whom* I bestow this honor. (I bestow it to *her,* not *she,* and it is part of a prepositional phrase.)

    b. **Example:** I will give the money back to *whomever* it belongs. (It belongs to *him,* not *he,* and is part of a prepositional phrase.)

    c. **Example:** Angela is the friend with whom I have dinner once a week. (I have dinner with *her,* not *she.*)

    d. **Example:** I decided to work for *whoever* paid the best.

(*He* paid the best. This is actually a subjective phrase, and "he'" is the agreement upon which you base the rule. You wouldn't say, "Him paid the best," and therefore you don't use *whomever* even though in this case it is within a prepositional phrase.)

____ **Pronouns:** Pronouns get really tricky when writing memoir. Your editor needs to pay really close attention to this and make sure that they don't confuse readers. If your editor doesn't know who you are talking about, use a noun instead in such a sentence.

Example of pronoun confusion: Trudy ate her breakfast and then went to visit her friend Marla. They went out for coffee and chatted for over an hour. She enjoyed the visit.

Correction: Trudy ate her breakfast and then went to visit her friend Marla. They went out for coffee and chatted for over an hour. Trudy enjoyed the visit.

____ **Sentence structure:** You need to keep your sentences clear but also add some beauty to them. One rule that works for me to keep sentences clear is "no more than two nouns and two verbs in one sentence." You can offer more of each and make it grammatically correct, but you run the risk of two things: (1) run-on sentences and (2) boring your reader. While keeping things concise, adding beauty that makes art is what really keeps your reader interested. Zora Neale Hurston does this so remarkably well, and I'll just offer a few of her quotes as examples.

"I have been in Sorrow's kitchen and licked out all the pots.

Then I have stood on the peaky mountain wrapped in rainbows, with a harp and a sword in my hands."

—Zora Neale Hurston

"I have the nerve to walk my own way, however hard, in my search for reality, rather than climb upon the rattling wagon of wishful illusions."

—Zora Neale Hurston

As discussed in the chapter on literary elements, she uses device to add beauty to her concise writing. Does your editor see and help you harness the art of the work? If not, she can you offer suggestions regarding literary elements and devices within your concise writing.

____ **Word choice:** Redundancy is using the same word often. You can consult a thesaurus to beef up your writing. As an editor, allow your emotions to tell you if you are interested in the story. Do you feel bored, preached to, engaged, or excited? Do you feel that the writer has used synonyms to accurately depict what he or she is writing about? If your editor isn't engaged in some way, he should offer feedback regarding word choice to help you. If he or she is confused, perhaps you used the wrong synonym out of the thesaurus to describe your passage.

Works Cited

Albom, Mitch. *Tuesdays with Morrie: An Old Man, a Young Man, and Life's Greatest Lesson*. New York: Doubleday, 1997.

Burlae, Krista. "Midwifery." *6th Annual Writer's Digest Short Short Story Competition: A Collection*. Victoria, BC: Trafford, 2006.

Burroughs, Augusten. *Running with Scissors: A Memoir*. New York: St. Martin's Press, 2002.

Cameron, Julia. *The Artist's Way: A Spiritual Path to Higher Creativity*. Los Angeles: Jeremy P. Tarcher/Perigee, 1992.

Dugard, Jaycee Lee. *A Stolen Life: A Memoir*. New York: Simon & Schuster, 2011.

Dyer, Wayne W. *Inspiration: Your Ultimate Calling*. Carlsbad, CA: Hay House, 2006.

Ford, Debbie. *The Dark Side of the Light Chasers: Reclaiming Your Power, Creativity, Brilliance, and Dreams*. New York: Riverhead Books, 1998.

King, Stephen. *Gerald's Game*. New York: Viking, 1992.

London, Jack. *The Call of the Wild*. New York: Macmillan, 1963.

Myss, Caroline M. *Sacred Contracts: Awakening Your Divine Potential*. New York: Harmony Books, 2001.

Peers, E. Allison. *Dark Night of the Soul*. Grand Rapids: Christian Classics Ethereal Library, 2003.

Picoult, Jodi. *My Sister's Keeper: A Novel*. New York: Washington Square Press, 2005.

Pressfield, Steven. *The War of Art: Winning the Inner Creative Battle*. New York: Rugged Land, 2002.

Ruiz, Miguel. *The Four Agreements: A Practical Guide to Personal Freedom*. San Rafael, CA: Amber-Allen Publishing, 1997.

Sebold, Alice. *The Lovely Bones*. Boston: Little, Brown, 2002.

Stahl, Jerry. *Permanent Midnight: A Memoir*. New York: Warner Books, 1995.

Tarantino, Quentin. *Pulp Fiction: A Quentin Tarantino Screenplay*. New York: Miramax Books/Hyperion, 1994.

Walls, Jeannette. *The Glass Castle: A Memoir*. New York: Scribner, 2005.

Zygielbaum, Joseph L. *The Odyssey of a Partisan: A Memoir*. Lincoln, NE: Arthur Zygielbaum, 2009.

Bio

Krista Burlae is the founder of Catharsis Writing Institute in New Mexico and author of the workbook, *The Art of Cathartic Memoir.* First a social worker in community mental health and hospice, she ultimately expanded her desire to help people to a wider audience by following her aspirations as a writer and entrepreneur. Her groundbreaking theory of violence prevention gained the attention of researchers around the globe upon its publication in 2004. Krista has published fiction and has won awards as a playwright. In 2006, she founded and guided a small business, *Writer's Wellspring,* editing several memoirs awaiting publication. She has taught psychology, sociology and college writing in academic settings, and for the general public. Catharsis Writing Institute offers writing workshops, coaches authors, ghost writes and edits books, specializing in memoir.

Other books and periodicals by Krista Burlae
and Catharsis Writing Institute

Catharsis Journal

50585322R00072

Made in the USA
San Bernardino, CA
27 June 2017